VALLEY FORGE

★ ★

VALLEY FORGE

 **DILLON PRESS**
New York

Maxwell Macmillan Canada
Toronto
Maxwell Macmillan International
New York   Oxford   Singapore   Sydney

by Libby Hughes

Photo Credits

Cover photo: R. Frear
Back photo: R. Frear
Frontispiece: Valley Forge National Historical Park
The Bettman Archive: 9, 11, 28, 38, 42, 47, 54; Valley Forge National Historical Park: 22, 24, 27, 49, 57, 62, 65, 66; Libby Hughes: 32, 34, 41

Library of Congress Cataloging-in-Publication Data

Hughes, Libby.
    Valley Forge / by Libby Hughes.
       p. cm. — (Places in American history)
    Summary: Describes George Washington's headquarters at Valley Forge, where he and his army of 12,000 men wintered beginning in December of 1777, and its significance for the American Revolution.
    ISBN 0-87518-547-9
    1. Valley Forge (Pa.)—History—Juvenile literature. 2. Washington, George, 1732-1799—Headquarters—Pennsylvania—Valley Forge—Juvenile literature. [1. Valley Forge (Pa.)—History. 2. United States—History—Revolution, 1775-1783. 3. Washington, George, 1732-1799.] I. Title. II. Series.
E234.H84   1993
973.3'341—dc20   92-23391

Dillon Press
Macmillan Publishing Company
866 Third Avenue
New York, NY 10022

Maxwell Macmillan Canada, Inc.
1200 Eglinton Avenue East
Suite 200
Don Mills, Ontario M3C 3N1

Macmillan Publishing Company is part of the Maxwell Communication Group of Companies.

First edition

Printed in the United States of America

10   9   8   7   6   5   4   3   2   1

CONTENTS

PLACES IN
AMERICAN
HISTORY

Valley Forge

N

Schuylkill River

Washington's
Headquarters

Washington Memorial
Chapel and Valley Forge
Historical Society Museum

Mount
Joy

Inner Line Drive

Inner Line Drive

North Gulph Road

**VALLEY FORGE NATIONAL
HISTORICAL PARK**

Grand Parade

County Line Road

Outer Line Drive

Visitor
Center

Valley Creek

Covered Bridge

Pennsylvania
Valley Forge

CHAPTER 1

RETREAT TO VALLEY FORGE

A vivid part of American history took place at Valley Forge, Pennsylvania. More than two centuries ago, George Washington and his troops retreated to these wooded hills 20 miles (32 kilometers) northwest of Philadelphia. The modern visitor can easily imagine the spirit of desperation during that memorable winter of 1777–1778.

Think of yourself as a soldier in the American Revolution. On December 19, 1777, you arrived with torn clothing and your feet wrapped in canvas or cowhide. Gazing over the slopes and hills, you would see the bare limbs of trees clawing at the sky. You would feel the harsh winds whipping across the military encampment and slashing at George Washington's 12,000 soldiers.

You would watch messengers and aides rushing in and out of George Washington's headquarters on the banks of the Schuylkill River.

Valley Forge was a turning point for the soldiers of the American Revolution. No battles were fought there, but the men who managed to endure the long winter left Valley Forge better trained. And, after six months at Valley Forge, a stronger Continental army emerged. The soldiers marched onward to become victorious in the fight for American independence from Great Britain.

One man was responsible for keeping the spirit of endurance alive among the soldiers at Valley Forge. He was George Washington, who had spent a long time in the military. His leadership was severely tested at Valley Forge. But he had been preparing for this moment since boyhood.

Long before George Washington became the first president of the United States in 1789, he was a land surveyor, a soldier, and, finally,

Winter at Valley Forge

commander in chief of the Continental army.

His father died when George was only 11 years old. His mother, Mary Ball Washington, taught her son religious and moral principles. Talented in mathematics, 16-year-old George selected land surveying as his profession. Apprenticed to landowners, he tramped over Virginia's hills and gullies, measuring large and small tracts of land.

Throughout boyhood, however, George Washington had a strong interest in warfare. His half brother Lawrence had gone off to war in the West Indies, leaving George and his school friends to play soldier with their wooden rifles while marching across the Virginia farmlands.

Young George joined the Virginia militia (like the National Guard) at age 21 to defend his home colony of Virginia and his country against the British, who wanted to control and dominate the American colonies.

In 1758, George returned to his responsibili-

General George Washington, painted by Charles Willson Peale

ties at his Mount Vernon estate in Virginia by resigning his commission from the French and Indian War. This war lasted from 1689 to 1763. The British and French were fighting over land in Canada and the American West. The Indians fought against both forces in defending their land on the borders and in the open frontiers. Washington had been sent to protest the seizure of land by the French.

Great Britain's domination over the colonies became stronger. Washington rejoined Virginia's volunteer militia in 1774. When Britain tried to impose greater taxation on its 13 colonies, the voice of protest spread across the colonies. The American revolutionary war began on April 19, 1775. On June 14, 1775, the American Congress quickly formed the Continental army, named for the European, or continental, influence on the American military. The very next day, George Washington was appointed its commander in chief.

The main attacks from the red-coated British army under Major General William Howe were fought in Massachusetts, New York, and on the borders of Canada. The Americans were outnumbered and poorly trained. During the year 1776, Washington and some of his troops moved south to New Jersey and crossed the Delaware River to face General Howe, who had landed by ship at New Brunswick, New Jersey. The Continental army spent the harsh winter of 1776–1777 at Morristown, New Jersey. Both sides waited for spring to engage in military confrontations.

Communication in those days was difficult. Riders on horseback carried letters from George Washington to his officers in the different colonies. For the British, the problems were even greater. The War Office in London gave the orders. But mail from England took six to eight weeks to arrive in America by ship.

Therefore, General Howe made some decisions on his own. George Washington waited to see what Howe would do in the summer of 1777. Since Howe controlled the seas, he sailed south to Maryland to try to take Philadelphia, the capital of the 13 states. On August 25, Howe landed at Elkton, Maryland. Howe's men were a combination of Britons and Hessians. The Hessians were from Germany and very well trained, but there was often friction between the two groups.

Nevertheless, they fought together against the American colonists. Washington sent his men down the Brandywine Creek to stop Howe from invading Philadelphia. But they couldn't. The Americans lost their battle at Brandywine, Pennsylvania, on September 11.

Endangered by staying in Philadelphia, the Continental Congress moved west to York, Pennsylvania. On September 18 they established temporary quarters there. They hid the Liberty Bell, which they had taken from Philadelphia, in Allentown, Pennsylvania. The 2,080-pound Liberty Bell, made in England, was kept in the State House (now know as Independence Hall) in 1752 to summon legislators to the Assembly.

Washington retreated northeast of Philadelphia, hoping to defend all points of entrance to the city. While he positioned most of his men near Germantown, Pennsylvania, the British were scouting for food. They heard that there was a gristmill full of flour, pork, and iron utensils at Valley Forge on Valley Creek.

Hearing of Howe's intentions, Washington sent Lieutenant Colonel Alexander Hamilton and Captain Henry Lee (father of Robert E. Lee) to load all the goods from the Valley Forge storehouses on barges and bring them north. But Howe assaulted Hamilton and Lee and took everything. The British burned the old ironworks at Valley Forge when they left on September 23.

Washington had left one division at Paoli, under the command of Brigadier General

Anthony Wayne—a wild and flamboyant American general. Wayne's men were ordered to stop the British from moving north. The colonists waited in a wooded valley, but the enemy surprised them, killing and wounding most of Wayne's men. This battle became known as the "Paoli Massacre."

After the Brandywine defeat and Paoli slaughter, Washington was eager for a victory. He pushed farther north to Germantown, which was a strategic point to guard the Delaware River. The British had spies among the local population and found out about the lay of the land there. False reports were delivered to George Washington, who sent Major General Nathanael Greene into the center of Germantown and into the heart of British troops. Greene expected military support to follow, but the weather was bad. Howe's troops encircled Greene's, nearly trapping them. Under heavy fog, Greene withdrew his men on

October 4. The Germantown battle was called a draw, although the British considered it a victory.

The Americans finally won a major battle at Saratoga, New York, on October 17. The Congress and American forces were overjoyed to hear news of British General John Burgoyne's defeat by General Horatio Gates. As Washington and his men retreated north of Philadelphia to Whitemarsh, the tired troops stationed themselves on the ridges. The American victory in New York lifted their spirits.

But Washington was thinking ahead. He sent Nathanael Greene back to the head of the Delaware River to capture and stand on the Fort Mercer peninsula and the mud island of Fort Mifflin.

At these two points, Washington planned to stonewall the British from moving along the Delaware River or coming down the Schuylkill River, which flows into the Delaware. However,

Howe's troops were too strong for Greene, and he had to retreat to Whitemarsh.

Full of confidence, the British attempted to draw Washington's troops into battle at Whitemarsh. With fatigued and footsore troops, Washington was reluctant to respond to Howe's bait. He kept his troops poised on the Whitemarsh ridges. Howe was afraid Washington might outnumber and overpower him. Therefore, Howe withdrew and headed back to Philadelphia.

While at Whitemarsh, Washington began to search for a winter encampment for his 12,000 men. Congress had refused to give him supplies and support at Whitemarsh because it was too close to Philadelphia. Congress wanted the Continental army safely distant but near enough to defend its capital.

On December 11, Washington broke camp at Whitemarsh and began a long march to the slopes at Valley Forge, where he thought there might be a good place to spend the winter.

CHAPTER 2

An Unforgettable Winter

Thousands of soldiers gathered their tents, rusting equipment, and heavy wagons to follow George Washington across the bumpy terrain of Pennsylvania. With elbows and knees jutting through threadbare clothing, the men waded through icy rivers and trudged for days to a place called Gulph Mills. After the British had abandoned it, the Continental army arrived.

At first, Washington thought this might be a suitable place for a winter encampment. He changed his mind and decided upon Valley Forge as a better location. It was nearly 20 miles (32 kilometers) northwest of Philadelphia. The triangular tract of land had 3,000 acres (1,215 hectares) of farmland and woods. Bordered by ridges and rivers, the site satisfied Washington's trained eye as a surveyor.

The hungry and bedraggled troops marched and limped to Valley Forge. The rain had made deep ruts in the road, which had frozen during the December days. Many of the men had worn through their shoes, and the frozen ruts cut their feet. George Washington said in a letter to the Continental Congress: "You might have tracked the army to Valley Forge by the blood of their feet."

The land now known as Valley Forge had been owned and occupied by private owners. Some of them were Quakers, a peaceful and quiet religious group. They lived and farmed on the hilly land. Many of them worked at the forge (ironworks) and gristmill on Valley Creek, owned by the wealthy Potts family. Unfortunately, the large forge had been raided and completely destroyed by the British.

When Washington and his men finally

reached Valley Forge on December 19, they were hungry, cold, and exhausted. The day before had been declared a day of thanksgiving by Congress, but the men had no food with which to celebrate. One soldier wrote in his diary that he had eaten a small piece of pumpkin that he fried on a rock.

The soldiers were ordered to pitch their tents on the hardened ground. Washington, too, set up the marquee tent (a commanding officer's tent with a canopy in the front) near the Artillery Park area. He slept inside the tent, but the canvas canopy covered his working table, where his aides and officers reported to him.

Washington knew the thin canvas tents would not keep the men warm enough throughout the winter. Washington's chief engineer, Brigadier General Louis Duportail, spent those first days scouting over the many acres of Valley Forge. He determined that huts for the more than 12,000 men and 350 officers could be easily

Washington's sleeping marquee

built on the warm sides of the hills.

    To keep the soldiers busy and less occupied with thoughts of food, Washington commanded them to start building more than 1,200 huts. Most of the horses had died or were too weak to haul the trees from the forests. Therefore, the men tied the logs together and dragged them to the building sites. Duportail had designed three avenues where the huts would be built. They nicknamed their makeshift military post "Logtown."

Thomas Paine, the famous writer and aide to Nathanael Greene, observed the feverish activity and commented in *The American Crisis*: "They appeared to me like a family of beavers; everyone busy. Some carrying logs, others mud, and the rest fastening them together."

The huts were very crude, measuring 16 by 14 feet (5 by 4 meters), and had no windows. Doors faced south and were covered by canvas or slabs of wood. Chimneys were placed anywhere—usually on the east side. Bunk beds were made of tree limbs and straw. Washington held a contest and offered a reward of $12 to the fastest hut built. Another reward went to the most original roof. Each hut had a pail and a plank for

Replicas of soldiers' huts at Valley Forge

a table. Bayonets were used as frying spatulas.
There were 12 men to a hut, and they nearly
choked from the smoke that could not escape
through because there were no windows. The
officers had only six or eight men to a hut.

Deeply disturbed by the desperate need for
food and clothing, Washington wrote Henry
Laurens, the president of the Congress at York,
on December 23: "I am now convinced, beyond a
doubt that unless some great and capital change
suddenly takes place in that line, this Army
must inevitably be reduced to one or other of
these three things. Starve, dissolve, or disperse,
in order to obtain subsistence in the best man-
ner they can; rest assured, Sir, this is not an
exaggerated picture, but that I have abundant
reason to support what I say."

Of the total number of men, 2,898 of them
were confined to their huts or sent to hospitals
in Yellow Springs, Lancaster, or Bethlehem. Two
or three larger huts served as hospitals at Valley

Forge. Of his men, Washington said to Laurens in that same letter: "Although they (Congress) seem to have little feelings for the naked and distressed soldier, I feel abundantly for them and from my soul pity those miseries while it is neither in my power to relieve or prevent."

The Potts family owned a small stone house at the corner of Valley Creek and Schuylkill River. Deborah Hewes, a cousin of the Pottses', agreed to rent it to George Washington for 100 pounds ($300). Instead of moving into the five-room, two-story house immediately, he stayed in his tent until early January. He would not leave there until most of the huts were built and the men were housed in warmer quarters. Then he moved into the house. Some of Washington's generals—Varnum, Knox, Stirling, Lafayette, Maxwell, Greene, and Huntington—lived with local families in farmhouses scattered over the post.

Despite the unbelievable hardships experienced by the men at Valley Forge, they respected

Isaac Potts's House, Washington's headquarters

Engraving of Washington visiting wounded soldiers at Valley Forge

and admired George Washington. Frequently, they referred to him as "His Excellency." Perhaps they sensed his concern for them.

After the huts were made, Duportail selected

strategic spots to fortify the triangular parcel of land. There was an outer line and an inner line where brigades were stationed for defense. Mount Joy was the highest point, at 400 feet (122 meters). Foxholes known as "redoubts" were dug. Instead of using sandbags, the soldiers made large barrels from limbs and twigs. They were stuffed with dirt, leaves, and straw and served as a barricade. Above the Schuylkill River was Huntington's brigade and the 24-hour guard duty, watching for suspicious movements from the British. Often, the feet of these guards were so cold they had to stand on their hats to keep them warm.

In the center of Valley Forge was a large flat stretch of land, called the Grand Parade, where the soldiers drilled and marched. The Artillery Park, commanded by Brigadier General Henry Knox, and its long line of cannons faced the Grand Parade.

The Christmas of 1777 was not a joyous

occasion. While the British were eating their beef, potatoes, and mince pies in the warmth of Philadelphia homes, the Continental army soldiers each had only a few spoonsful of rice and fire cake (fried flour and water) and two ounces of grog (liquor) to celebrate. Washington and 15 of his aides and officers had some vegetables, veal, and mutton. But Washington worked most of the day, writing letters filled with orders and requests.

The temperature ranged from 26 to 34°F (-3 to 1°C). By Christmas night, it had snowed, leaving 4 inches (10 centimeters) on the ground. Some of the men played cards and dice (made from empty bullets). This was one Christmas that George Washington and 12,000 of his men would never forget.

CHAPTER 3

Dealing with Congress

On the banks of Valley Creek and only steps from the shallow Schuylkill River was Washington's sandy-stoned headquarters, flanked by sycamore, hickory, and Spanish oak trees. The headquarters was the nerve center for the revolutionary war. The problems at Valley Forge were only a fraction of Washington's responsibilities. He directed and communicated with his forces in New England, New York, New Jersey, Virginia, Delaware, and Pennsylvania.

The narrow hallway of the headquarters was always crowded and bustling with official visitors coming and going. In the two small rooms downstairs, Washington and his nine aides wrote many letters by hand. There was hardly a

Aides' office at George Washington's headquarters

quiet moment for the tall commander in chief.

Upstairs, Washington, some of his officers, and his aides squeezed into three small bedrooms. The kitchen was attached outside, with a large fireplace and kettles. Some of the servants slept on the kitchen floor at night. A separate

dining room was built behind the headquarters.
Some distance beyond that were the huts for
Washington's own special life guards, or military
bodyguards.

On January 1, 1778, Washington wrote again
to Henry Laurens, requesting assistance for his
men. Laurens replied: "My heart is full, my eyes
overflow when I reflect upon a camp 1/4 and
more of invalids for want of necessary covering—
an Army on the very verge of bankruptcy. For
want of food—that we are starving in the midst
of plenty—perishing by cold, and surrounded by
clothing sufficient for two Armies, but
uncollected . . . ."

The major obstructions to supplying food and
clothing to Washington's soldiers were bad
weather and lack of transportation. Plenty of
clothing was available in Connecticut, but get-
ting it to Valley Forge by wagon was almost
impossible. The British intercepted cattle and
wagonloads of flour. The shortage of horses to

Detached kitchen at George Washington's headquarters

pull the heavy wagons was also a problem.
When the food did arrive, much of the pork and
flour was spoiled and unfit to eat. Cattle, herded
to Valley Forge over many miles, were too thin
for beef.

The local farmers took their goods into Philadelphia and sold them to the British because they were paid in gold. The Continental army was short of money and gave the sellers vouchers. At the far corners of his military post, Washington established local markets for purchasing food on different days.

Foraging parties of 8 to 21 men scouted the countryside for food. Washington warned against seizing or stealing food from local people, but some of that happened anyway. Individual soldiers trapped squirrels, raccoons, and opossums. During the most desperate starvation times, the soldiers would shout from their huts, "No meat . . . no soldier."

General Varnum told George Washington, "The men have to be supplied, or they cannot be commanded." From Rhode Island, Varnum was considered very intelligent and well respected. He recruited more blacks than any other regiment. The total number who fought in the revolutionary war was 755. A Hessian in the British army wrote, "No regiment among the Americans is to be seen in which there are not Negroes in abundance and among them are able-bodied, strong and brave fellows." Even the British army employed blacks, but not as soldiers.

John Laurens of South Carolina asked his father to allow an all-black regiment of 5,000 men to be formed. But Henry Laurens had too many pressing issues as president of the Congress to consider his idealistic son's proposal.

On top of all the food troubles, there was a secret attempt to replace George Washington as commander in chief. This was called "Conway's Cabal." A cabal is a secret plot or political intrigue. General Thomas Mifflin, quartermaster general, was one of the leaders of this plan. Thomas Conway and Horatio Gates were also behind the plot. These two men had been responsible for the victory at Saratoga, after which Conway had been appointed inspector

general of the Continental army. Because George
Washington had lost the battles at Germantown
and Brandywine, Conway told members of
Congress that Washington was not capable of
being commander in chief. He suggested that
General Horatio Gates was more qualified for
that position.

Gates and Conway tried to bypass Washington and go directly to Congress with military
information. Washington's men objected.
Marquis de Lafayette, one of Washington's officers, insisted everything had to go through
Washington. Finally, the plot collapsed, and
Congress agreed to support George Washington.

To answer Washington's pleas about the
hardships of his army, Congress sent a committee of six to report to them about the general's
needs at Valley Forge. They arrived on January
24, 1778, and stayed through March. Settled in 2
miles (3 kilometers) from Washington's headquarters, the committee members saw with their

A painting of George Washington and General Lafayette at Valley Forge

own eyes the terrible conditions, but they didn't know how to assemble a report. Washington and his aides prepared 38 pages of a detailed analysis of the food rations, clothing supplies, and general attitude of the men.

Through the committee, Washington told Congress: "Our hopes are not placed in any particular city or spot of ground, but in preserving a good army, furnished with proper necessaries, to take advantage of favorable opportunities, and master and defeat the enemy piecemeal."

Washington also drew up a pension plan for his soldiers and officers. Some of his men were three months behind in their pay and had to use their own money. He said that after the war they should receive half pay. The debate in Congress offered no final conclusions to his proposals. He hoped the committee would see the need for military pensions.

There is a legendary story about George Washington at Valley Forge, one that has been regarded with skepticism by historians. During the desperate few months at the winter encampment, Washington reportedly disappeared from his headquarters and walked to the edge of a wooded area. There, he knelt down in the snow and prayed for God's help for his men. Isaac Potts, the owner of the land around the headquarters, had come to speak with Washington. When Potts saw Washington in a praying position, he quietly walked away to leave the commander in chief alone.

The only documentary evidence for this story came from Washington's first biographer, the Reverend Mason L. Weems, who claimed that Isaac Potts had repeated the event to him. There is also evidence that Washington was a religious man and often prayed an hour every night in his home at Mount Vernon. A large Bible was alongside his four-poster bed in one of the upstairs rooms at headquarters. He also encouraged his men to turn to God's guidance and care for help.

Bronze Freedom Foundation statue of Washington praying at Valley Forge

Martha Washington

CHAPTER 4

VON STEUBEN SHAPES THE ARMY

February brought two signs of hope for George Washington and his men at Valley Forge. They were the arrival of Martha Washington, George's wife, and Baron von Steuben, a Prussian captain.

Martha Washington left the comfort of her home and estate at Mount Vernon, Virginia, to stay with her husband through the bitter winter months at his headquarters. Her very presence gave him greater peace and confidence for the future. Even the men seemed to respond to the presence of Martha Washington. When she toured the encampment, the men tried to present a cleaner and more mannerly appearance.

There were other women on the post. Some were called "camp followers." They were wives,

mothers, and sisters who followed their soldiers
and officers. Some of these women stayed in the
huts while others boarded with local families.
They did the laundry, cooking, sewing, and nursing. Those with nursing experience were actu-
ally paid for tending to the sick.

Mrs. Nathanael Greene had come in January.
She was a great favorite among the officers.
Catherine Greene spoke French and communicated fluently with some of Washington's aides
and European officers. Lord Stirling's wife and
daughter stayed in his quarters, and Mrs. Henry
Knox arrived in May.

More social gatherings and events took place
after Martha's arrival. Usually, there were 14 or
15 men at Washington's dinner table. They were
his aides and key officers. Two or three times a
week, Martha would expand her guest list to 20
or 25. Sometimes, she would arrange for music
in the evenings, as she did on her husband's
birthday, February 22, 1778. A group of fife and

drummers from the artillery brigade came to headquarters to serenade General Washington on his 46th birthday.

Within the cramped headquarters, the men arranged a sitting room for the commander's wife. Here, she was said to have sewed and knitted socks and gloves for some of the men. Although she did not directly nurse the ailing soldiers, she made arrangements for their care by the local women at the camp hospitals.

The day after Washington's birthday, a stout Prussian officer presented himself at Washington's headquarters. He was Friedrich Wilhelm Ludolf Gerhard Augustin Baron von Steuben. He had presented his credentials to the Congress at York on February 3.

Von Steuben had met Benjamin Franklin in Paris and asked Franklin if he could serve in the Continental army. Although von Steuben had only been a captain in the service of Frederick the Great of Prussia, Franklin gave him the rank of lieutenant general with a list of grand achievements to impress the Congress. As a professional soldier, von Steuben was looking for a military cause. The revolutionary war suited his purposes.

When von Steuben arrived and offered his services as a volunteer, George Washington was suspicious at first. Von Steuben told the commander that he would work without rank and only expect his expenses to be paid. Washington agreed. He named him acting inspector general.

After von Steuben toured the encampment and witnessed the miseries of the men, he said, "The men were literally naked, some of them in the fullest extent of the word. The officers who had coats had them of every color and make. I saw officers at a grand parade at Valley Forge mounting guard in a sort of dressing gown made of an old blanket or woolen bed cover."

The plump, 47-year-old Prussian wielded his

A painting of Baron von Steuben drilling soldiers at Valley Forge

cane on the parade grounds and gave orders in French or German. His language was explosive and his behavior colorful. The men found him a humorous character and poked fun at him. However, they came to respect his ability to train them.

Von Steuben's major contribution to the training of the Valley Forge men was the shift from the British military system to the French. The British moved their men in long, straight lines. They pointed their muskets (long-barreled firearms) at the object and fired. The French aimed through a range finder before firing. The French also moved in shorter lines that were quicker and more maneuverable.

Like a tough sergeant, von Steuben taught each man individually until a brigade inspector learned and could teach his own regiment, platoon, and company leaders. Von Steuben took Washington's 46 life guards first and instructed them in the new system. He added another 100 men to their ranks.

The Prussian was very demanding. He insisted the soldiers be clean shaven and presentably dressed during their drills. He taught them how to wage bayonet assaults. Until then, the soldiers' knowledge of bayonets was limited to spearing their meat for frying.

The Valley Forge troops gained uniformity and competence under von Steuben's instruction. He formed them into four columns abreast and

Modern-day photo of soldiers marching onto Grand Parade

reduced their marching steps from 120 to 75 per minute. This was a more normal pace. In order to keep in perfect step, he told them to watch the officer at the head of the column rather than the soldier in front. In two weeks, he taught them to bear arms, march, wheel, form columns, deploy, and execute. The words *ready, aim, fire* came from the von Steuben technique. The literal translation from French was "present," "take sight," and "fire."

When von Steuben began training, he decided to write a drill manual that could be used in the future. During the day, he put the men through basic training. At night, he wrote the day's set of instructions in French to be translated by Pierre Duponceau and revised by Alexander Hamilton and John Laurens—Washington's aides. They wrote von Steuben's drill manual into a blue book that was published in 1778. It became a standard book for military schools and academies.

John Laurens, the son of Henry Laurens—president of Congress—wrote his father: "Our men are the best crude materials for soldiers I believe in the world, for they possess a docility, and patience which astonish foreigners—with a little more discipline, we should drive the haughty Briton to his ships."

With the advent of spring, the spirit of the troops lifted. They drilled on the Grand Parade with pride and precision. Congress had appointed General Nathanael Greene as quartermaster general. Through his organization and efforts, clothing and food supplies began to flow into the camp. Once the ice melted on the shallow Schuylkill River, schools of fish were so abundant that the men could wade and scoop them into pails.

The men were glad to emerge from their smoke-filled huts and breathe the fresh air. For recreation, they played the British game of cricket. Mrs. Washington even arranged for a stage play or two to be performed in the bakehouse near headquarters. The bakehouse served as a courthouse for court martials on other occasions.

The Continental army was prepared to engage in battle. The soldiers were now disciplined and well-trained. The hardships and trials of Valley Forge were nearly over.

CHAPTER 5

THE FRENCH BACK THE AMERICANS

Twice a day von Steuben drilled the army. On April 6, he gave an exhibition on the Grand Parade, showing George Washington that in less than six weeks his army of volunteers could match the British, French, or any other army.

Some of the generals and many of the soldiers were eager to meet the enemy in battle. The boredom of winter was past and their new training gave them confidence. But George Washington felt the time was not right for a move out of camp. He encouraged the daily maneuvers as a means for readiness. Besides, soldiers from the North—some of whom were sick—were arriving in large numbers.

Meanwhile, in France, Benjamin Franklin

had been working diplomatically to persuade the French to support the Americans in their cause for independence. France had seen almost 100 years of greedy dictatorship through the reigns of King Louis XIV and King Louis XV. Since 1774 King Louis XVI had been the new ruler. He even considered a national assembly and a new constitution. The king's wife, Marie Antoinette, was a very strong and powerful influence on her husband. Benjamin Franklin befriended her on many social occasions. Both she and her husband listened sympathetically to Franklin's request for France's backing.

Because the French were angry with the British for pushing them out of Canada, King Louis favored siding with the Americans. Many of their professional soldiers crossed the ocean to join the cause against the British.

In early May, Benjamin Franklin signed a French alliance, declaring France's approval of America's desire for independence. When the

A portrait of Benjamin Franklin by Joseph S. Duplessis

news reached Valley Forge, a feeling of absolute joy swept through the encampment. George Washington said, "No news was received with more heartfelt joy." Morale had never been so high.

To celebrate, Washington said, "It becomes us to set apart a day for gratefully acknowledging the Divine Goodness, and celebrating the important event which we owe to his benign interposition. . . ."

On May 6, 1778, a *feu de joie* was declared. In French this means a day of rejoicing. Von Steuben planned the festivities for that day. At 9:00 A.M. George and Martha Washington, together with the generals and their wives, heard a sermon delivered by the Reverend W. Hunter. A cannon called the men to arms at 10:00 A.M. Washington reviewed the entire corps at noon and watched the drill parades on the Grand Parade. The whole army was set in two lines. The front line fired from right to left while those

Soldiers on parade at Valley Forge today

in the second line fired from left to right. When Washington left the celebration at 5:00 P.M., the troops shouted together, "Long live General Washington."

Many toasts were delivered at George Washington's table that night. Washington honored Baron von Steuben by giving him the rank of major general and praising his months of training.

During the spring, Britain's General Howe resigned and returned to England. He was replaced by General Henry Clinton. The news of the French alliance changed the British strategy. The British decided it was more important to defend the sugar islands in the West Indies from the French than to pursue a full-blown war against the Americans. Therefore, the British pulled out of Philadelphia.

Washington was not aware of the British plans. He sent small brigades east of the Schuylkill River to stand guard. When Washington heard the British were leaving Philadelphia on June 18, he directed the three final divisions of the Continental army to march out of Valley Forge on June 19, 1778.

Pursuing the British to Monmouth, New Jersey, Washington was ready for battle. However, his officer in charge, Charles Lee, wanted to withdraw. Washington ordered Lee to return to battle. By then, Clinton had time to bring reinforcements. As a result, there was no clear-cut victory at the Monmouth courthouse.

Meanwhile, Clinton marched his soldiers to New York City. For two years, Washington hovered over the British forces from White Plains, New York. In 1781, the last major battle of the Revolution was fought at Yorktown, Virginia, where the Americans were victorious over the British. The American Revolution ended in 1783.

Since no major battle was fought at Valley Forge, its significance was a victory for the American character rather than a military one. It was a winter encampment for 12,000 hungry, tired, and threadbare soldiers. The sacrifice and spirit of endurance exercised by these men have roused the emotions of Americans for more than two centuries. Had it not been for von Steuben and his method of military training, the outcome

of the revolutionary war might have been different. If the French had not supported American
independence, things might also have turned out
differently. Had George Washington, with his
strong leadership, not been in charge, almost
surely the war would have developed in an
entirely different way.

CHAPTER 6

VALLEY FORGE TODAY

The spirit of Valley Forge lives today. Several miles from the Pennsylvania Turnpike, the steep slopes, forests, and stone farmhouses from two centuries past are maintained under the United States Department of the Interior as the Valley Forge National Historical Park. In 1893, Valley Forge became a state park until July 1976, when the Department of the Interior assumed official responsibility.

When a bus or car first enters the park, it winds down to a parking lot and a modern Visitor Center, constructed in 1976 of granite and tinted glass. Seven flags from the American revolutionary war hang over the entrance. Administrative offices are on the second floor

The Visitor Center at Valley Forge

and in old Pennsylvania houses of the historical period. Almost 60 people work full-time at the park, with another 50 in the summer. Some of the seasonal staff dress in 18th-century costumes, depicting soldiers or female camp followers. Tourists may ask them questions about their firearms or anything about the winter of 1777–1778.

Inside the Visitor Center are cushioned couches, where visitors may watch a 15-minute video of Valley Forge's history. Except for a small bookstore, the main floor is devoted to displays of firearms, swords, and revolutionary accessories collected by George C. Neumann. The canvas marquee tent, belonging to George Washington while at Valley Forge, dominates the room.

With either a map or audiotape or both, the visitor then heads for a self-guided tour of the 3,200 acres. From May through September, visitors may choose a guided bus tour.

The grounds are not commercialized. They are clipped and mown by a grounds maintenance division. Since the park is now a recreation area for walking, running, biking, and picnicking, there are six miles of paved walkways and ten miles of horse trails. The road for cars and buses is woven into the triangular parcel of land around the Grand Parade. To view the military encampment of George Washington's day, the network of roads travels to the outer and inner defenses, the redoubts, and to the far corner, where Washington's headquarters still stands.

The monuments, statues, and huts are tastefully displayed throughout the rolling hills. At a high point is the Memorial Arch, dedicated in 1917 to the Valley Forge soldiers for their "patience and fidelity" during the famous winter. A bronze statue of Anthony Wayne mounted on his horse is not far from the arch. Near General Varnum's quarters is a statue of the famous von Steuben.

On the outer edges of the park are the stone farmhouses where Washington's senior officers lived with local families. Today, they are identified as Varnum's Quarters, Lafayette's Quarters, Maxwell's Quarters, Lord Stirling's Quarters, Knox's Quarters, and Huntington's Quarters.

NAKED AND STARVING AS THEY ARE
WE CANNOT ENOUGH ADMIRE
THE INCOMPARABLE PATIENCE AND FIDELITY
OF THE SOLDIERY

National Memorial Arch, dedicated in 1917 to the Valley Forge soldiers

General Varnum's quarters, the oldest park structure

These are not open to the public because some of them are rented to park administrators. There is one exception—the Horace Wilcox Memorial Library, on the site of Maxwell's Quarters. Now it is a reference library with 5,000 books relating to Valley Forge and the American revolutionary war. This library is open to the public two days a week.

None of the original huts from Washington's encampment survived. Only the depressions in the earth showed the park authorities where some of the 1,200 huts were located. Today, there are 35 replicas of the crude huts built by the soldiers from trees and mud.

One monument, not administered by the park, is the Washington Memorial Chapel and Museum, inspired by the Reverend W. Herbert Burk and built in 1905 on private property. It is part of the tour. The Valley Forge Historical Society operates the Museum.

The Isaac Potts house, known as George

Washington's headquarters, is one of the favorite sites to visit. On the banks of Valley Creek and only steps from the Schuylkill River is the double-story, sandy-stoned house. A park attendant is in the narrow hallway to explain the details of the rooms downstairs and upstairs.

One can almost imagine George Washington poised over his desk with his quill pen, scratching orders to his officers. In the entryway, a courier was probably sipping a cup of hot tea as he waited to mount his horse and carry Washington's messages across the snow and ice. The headquarters has been described as a small pentagon of military activity during the American Revolution.

Somehow, Valley Forge still throbs with the memory of patriotism and fortitude of the 1777–1778 winter. The winter winds almost carry the voices of the Continental army or the thunder of the cannons from Artillery Park.

Valley Forge: A Historical Time Line 1777 to 1778

September 11, 1777
The British under General Howe defeat George Washington's troops at Brandywine, Pennsylvania.

September 18, 1777
The British capture Philadelphia and the Congress moves to York, Pennsylvania.

October 4, 1777
General Howe almost traps Washington's troops at Germantown, Pennsylvania. The Continental army retreats under thick fog.

October 17, 1777
General Horatio Gates wins the battle of Saratoga against Britain's General John Burgoyne.

November 4 to December 11, 1777
Washington retreats to Whitemarsh, 11 miles (18 kilometers) north of Philadelphia.

December 19, 1777
Washington and his 12,000 men arrive at Valley Forge.

December 23, 1777
Washington writes a now-famous letter to Congress: ". . . this Army must inevitably starve, dissolve, or disperse . . ."

January 1778
"Conway's Cabal," an attempt to replace Washington with Horatio Gates, fails.

January 24 to March 12, 1778
The Congressional Committee visits Valley Forge.

February 3, 1778
Martha Washington stays until June.

February 22, 1778
George Washington turns 46 years old.

February 23, 1778
Baron von Steuben arrives to train and discipline troops.

March 17, 1778
Von Steuben trains Washington's life guards. Von Steuben writes a drill manual.

April 1778
Food, supplies, and clothing arrive.

May 6, 1778
French alliance supports American Independence. Howe resigns his post.

June 18, 1778
The British withdraw from Philadelphia.

June 19, 1778
Washington's men leave Valley Forge to pursue the British in New Jersey.

June 28, 1778
Neither Americans nor Britons win the Monmouth battle.

October 17, 1781
The last engagement of the American Revolution is won by the Americans at Yorktown, Virginia. September 3, 1783 Treaty of Paris recognizes American independence.

Visitor Information

Hours:

8:30 A.M. to 5:00 P.M.

Tours:

There is a bus tour from May to September.
Or you can rent an audiotape and tour Valley
Forge by car year-round. A self-guided tour from
a marked map takes tourists to Washington's
headquarters, the Grand Parade, Artillery
Parade, and other historical sights.

There are three picnic areas: Varnum's,
Wayne's Woods, and Betzwoods. A 6-mile (10-
kilometer) bike, jogging, and walking trail is
open to the public as well as 12 miles (20 kilometers) of horse trails. Boating on the Schuylkill
River is available. With a Pennsylvania sport
fish license, fishing is allowed. Pets on leashes
are permitted.

Visitor Center:

Open 8:30 A.M. to 5:00 P.M. daily. A 15-minute
film on the Valley Forge events is shown every
30 minutes 7 days a week. A museum and gift
shop are inside the center.

For further information write to:

The Superintendent
Valley Forge National Historical Park
Valley Forge, Pennsylvania 19481

INDEX